Madala
Adult Coloring Book

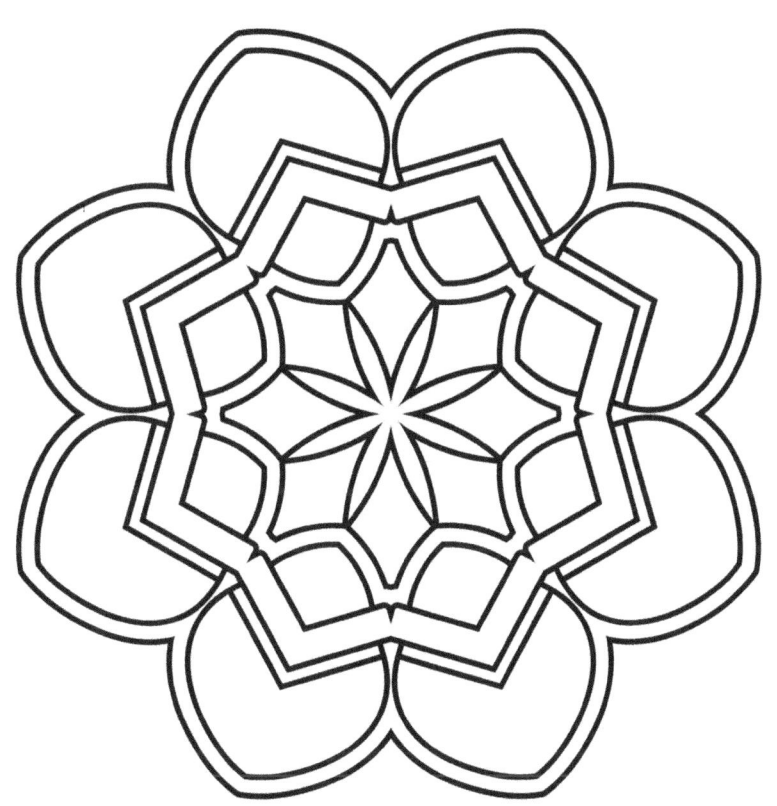

Belinda L. Frazier

Mandala
Adult Coloring Book
Stress Relieving For Beginner

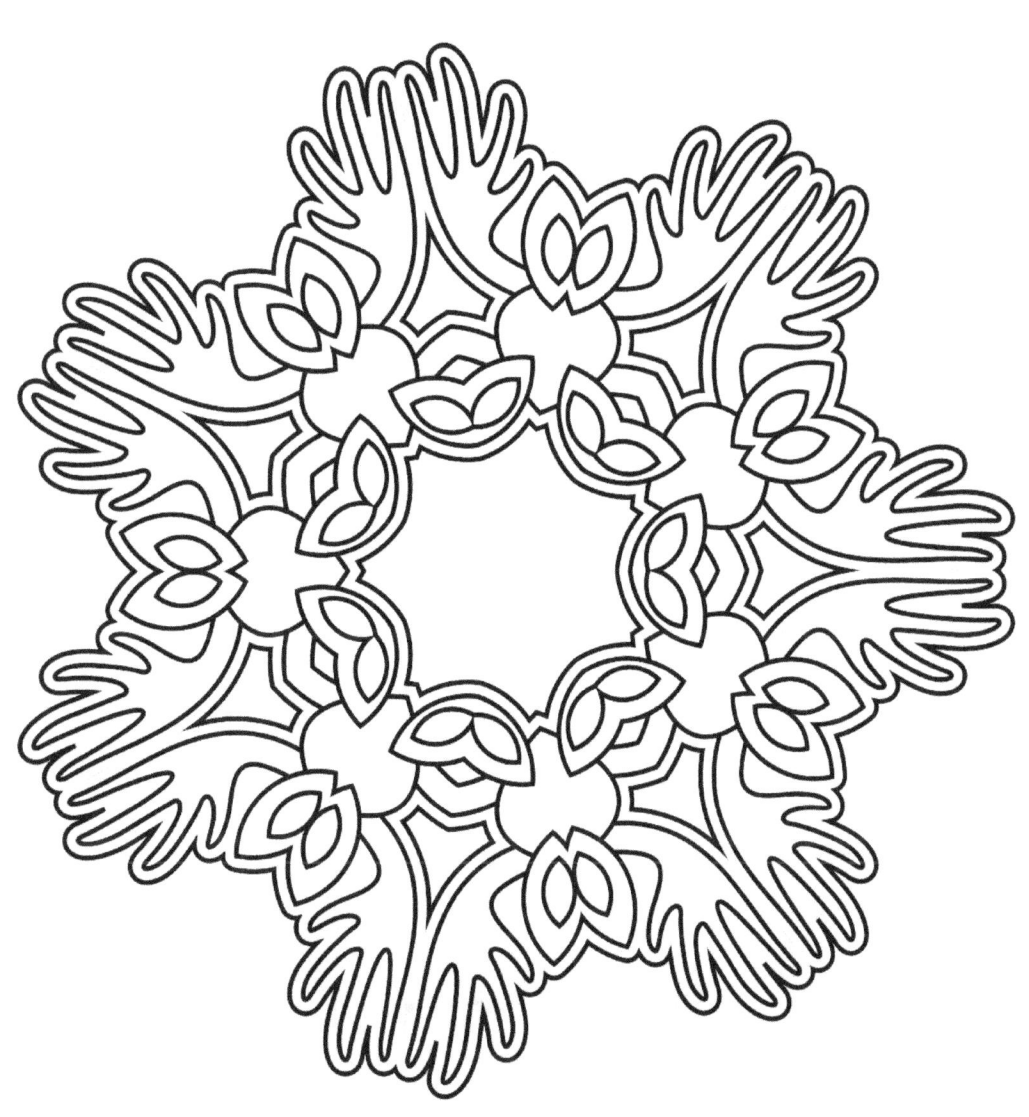

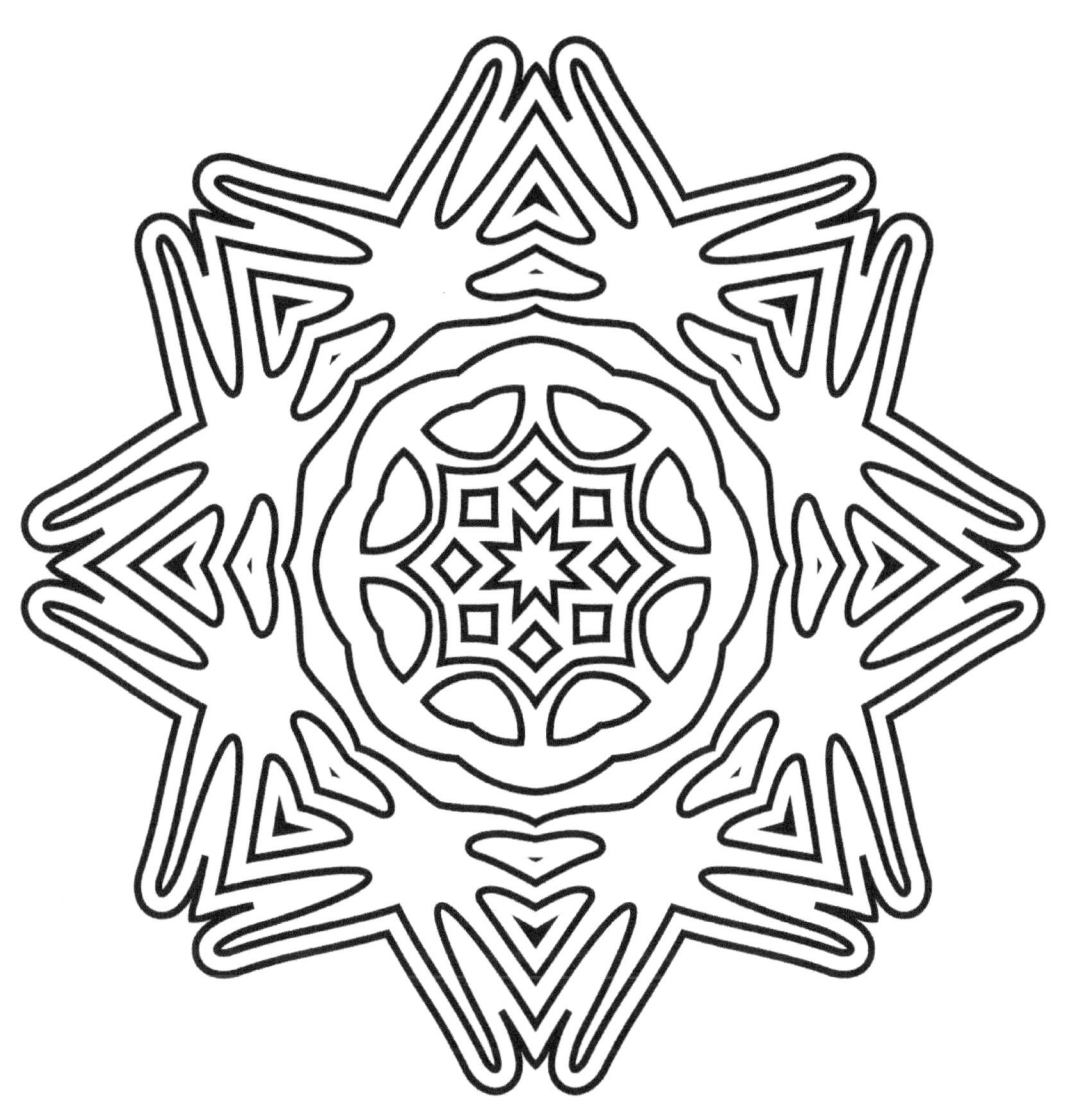

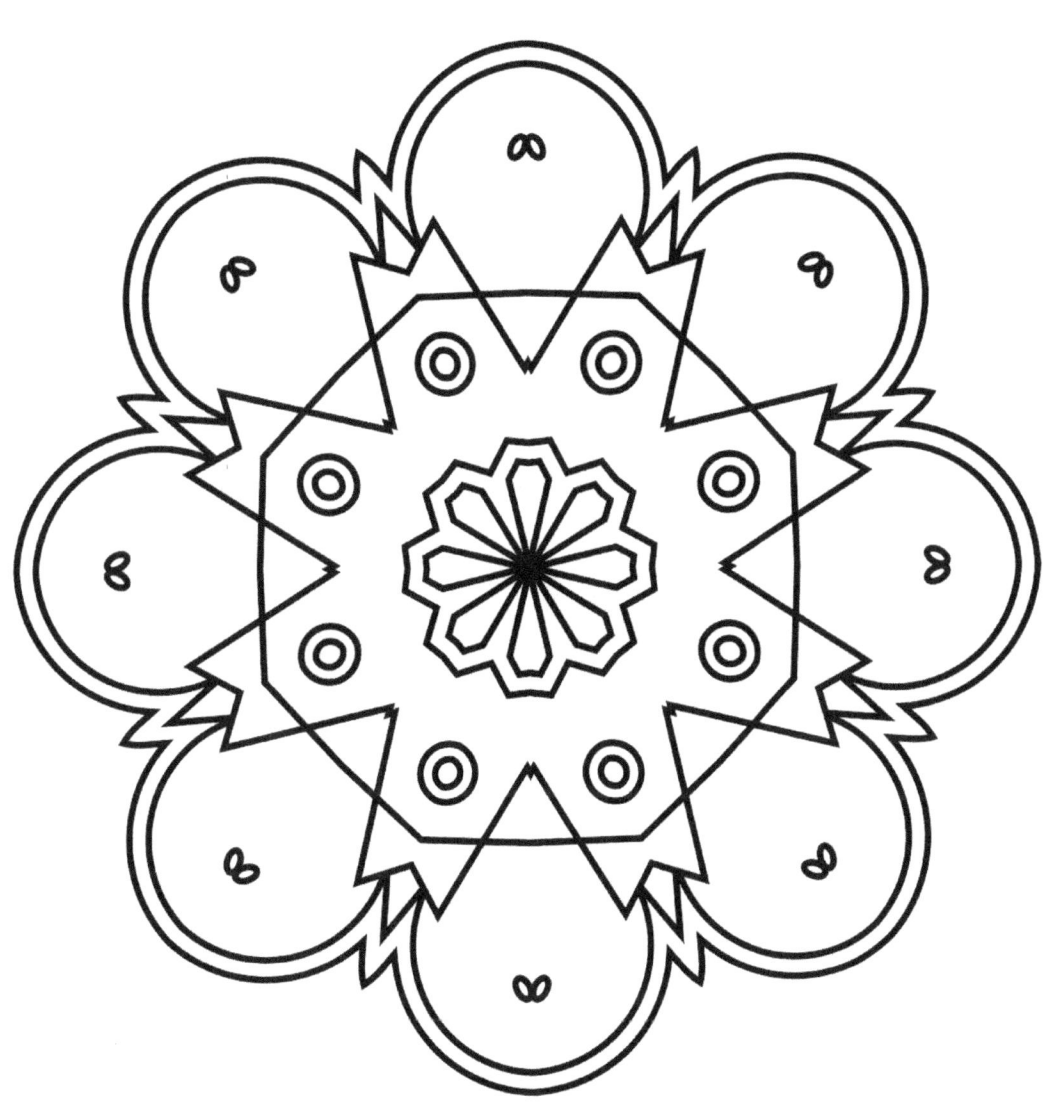

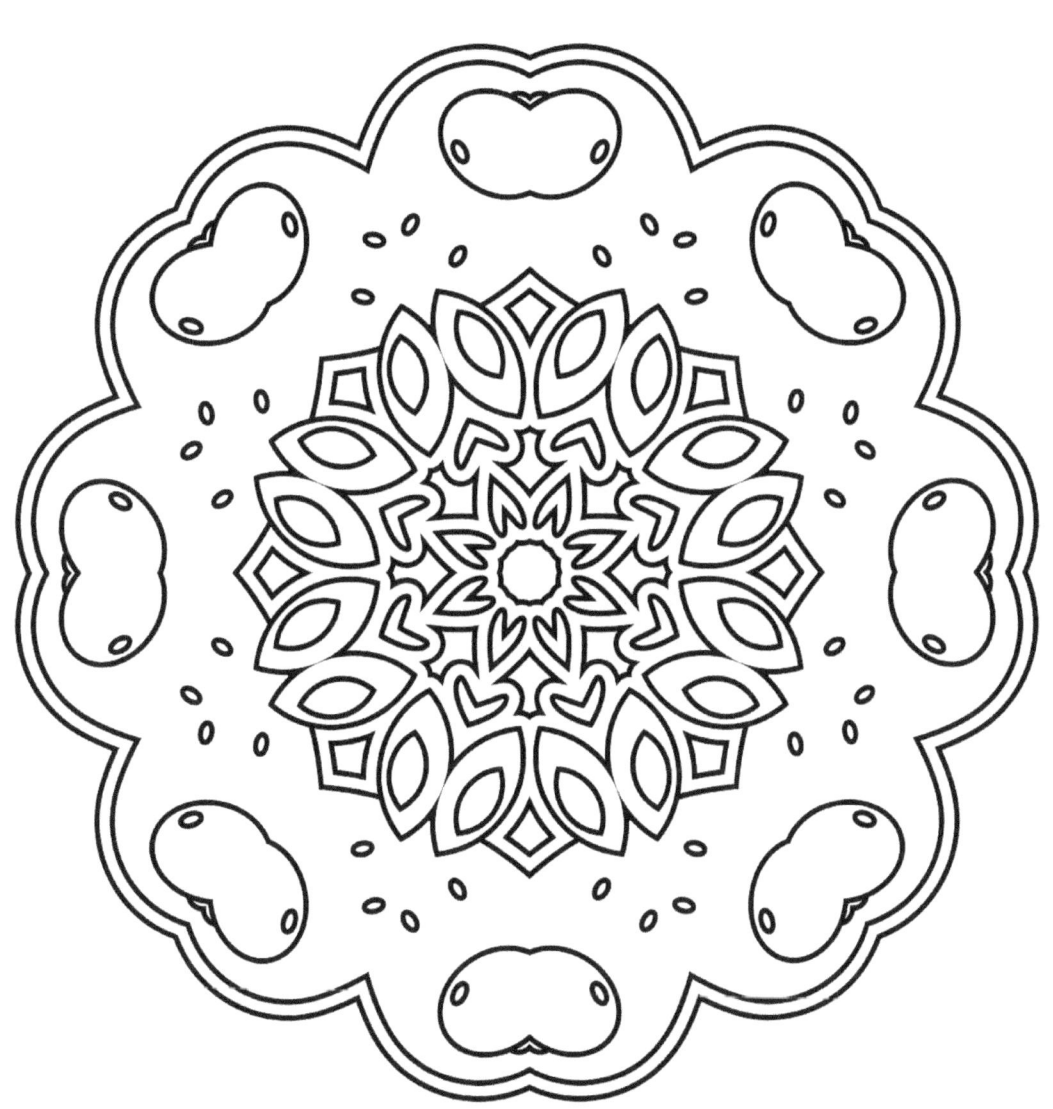

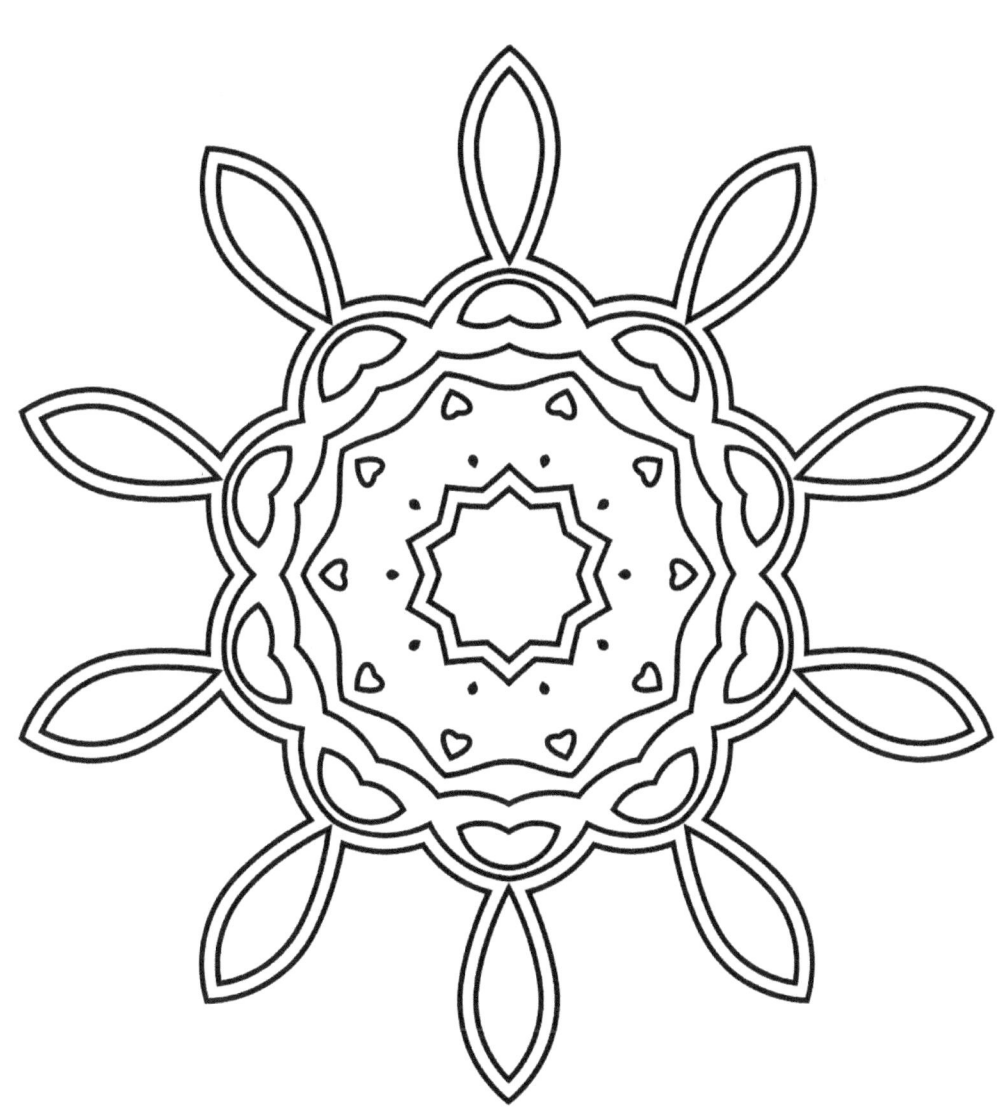

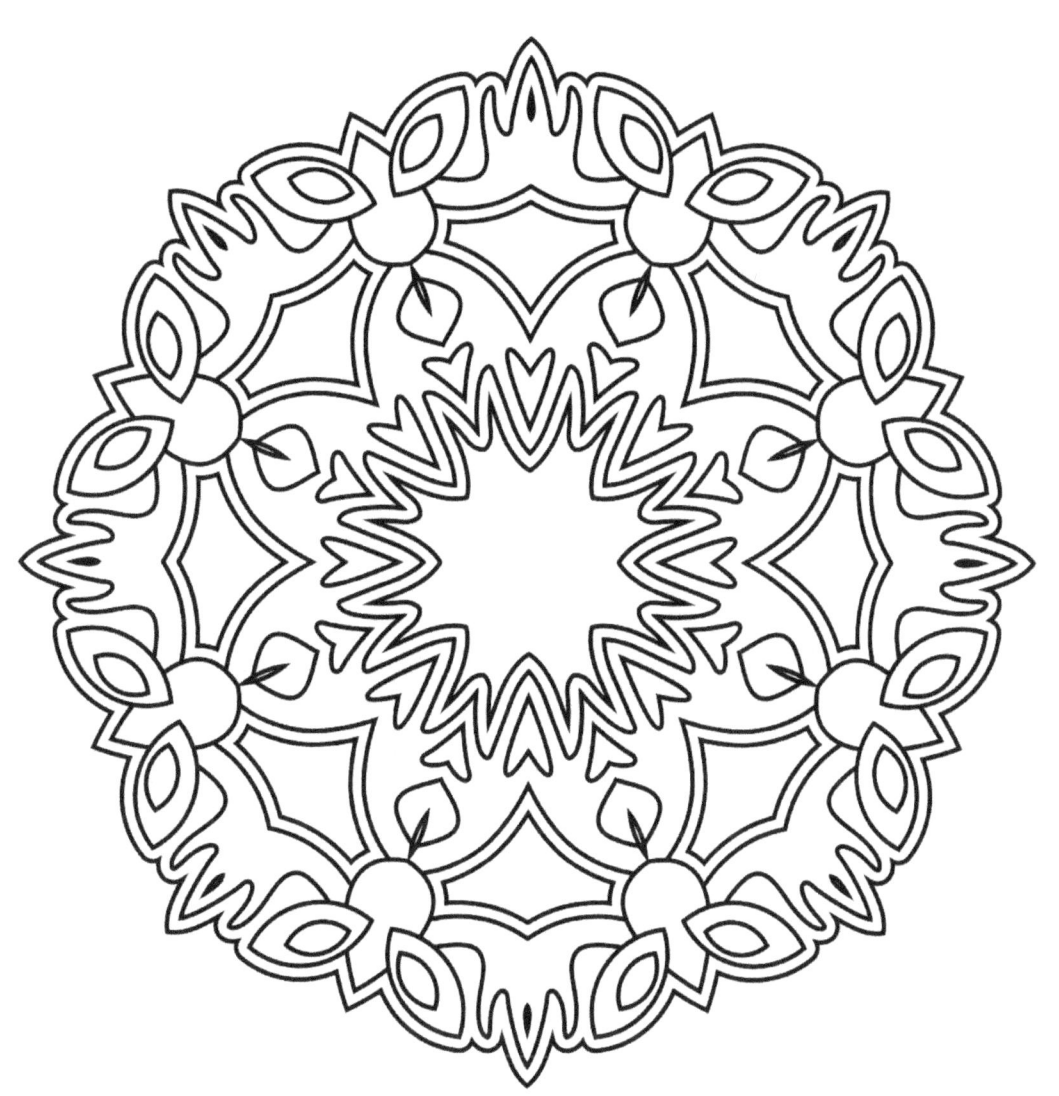

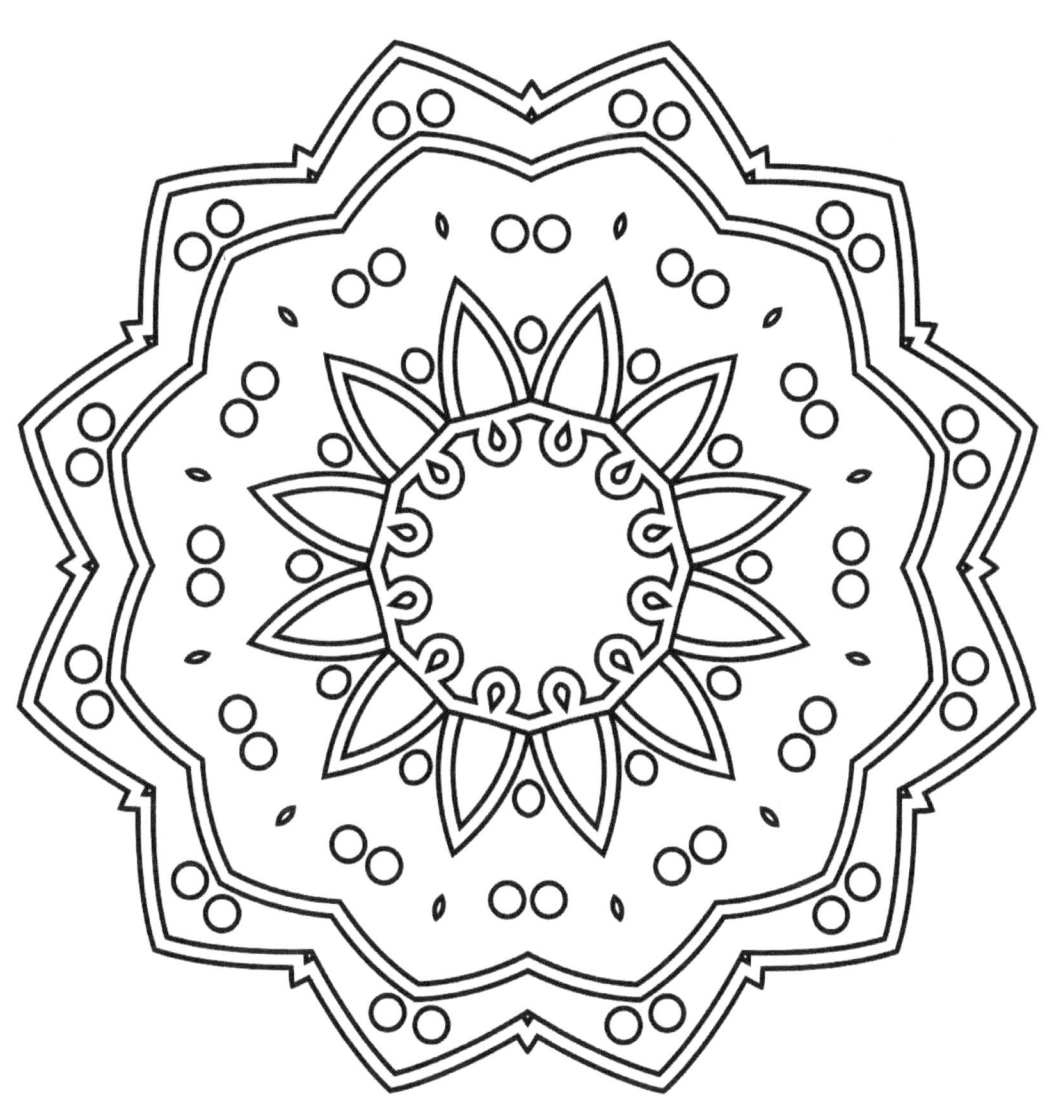

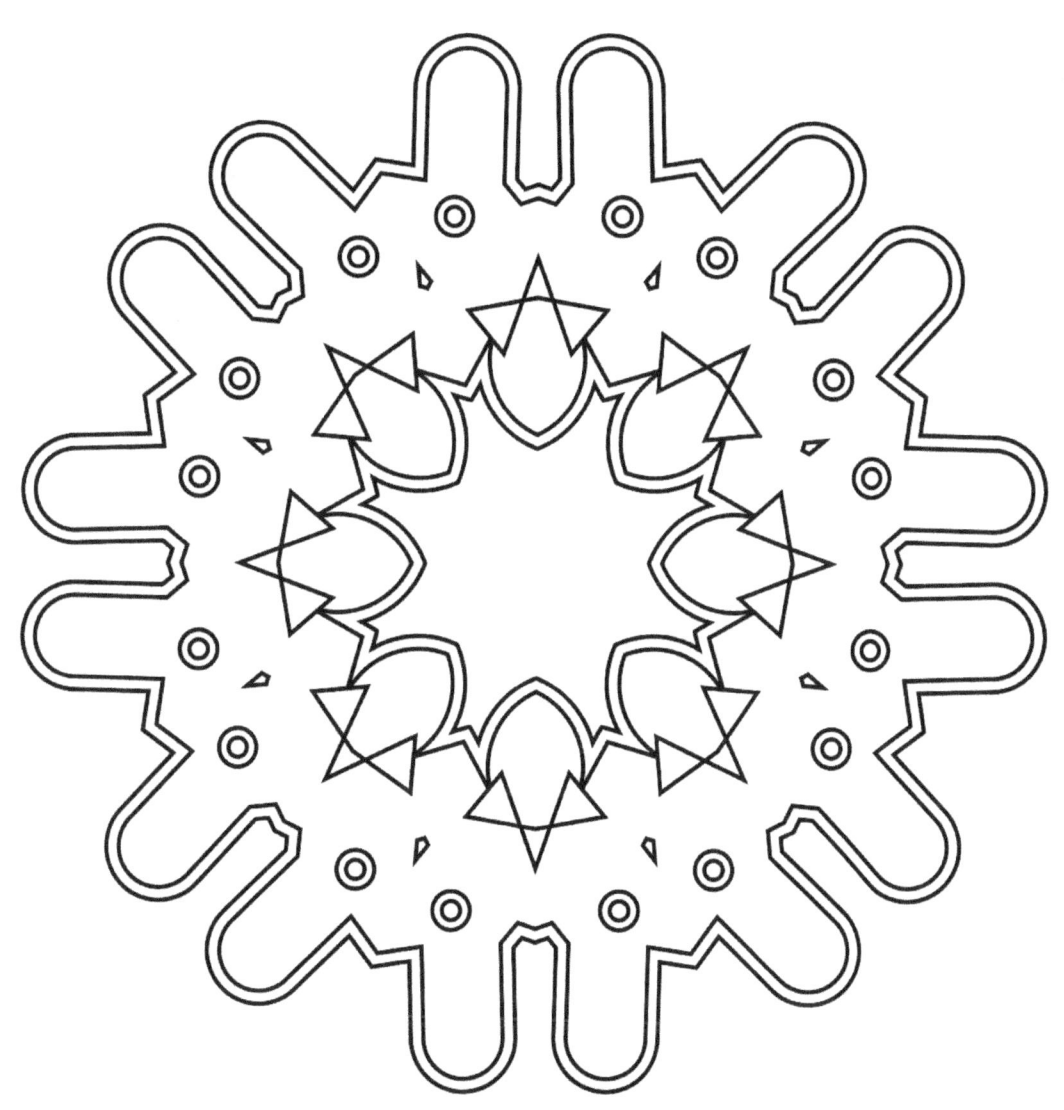

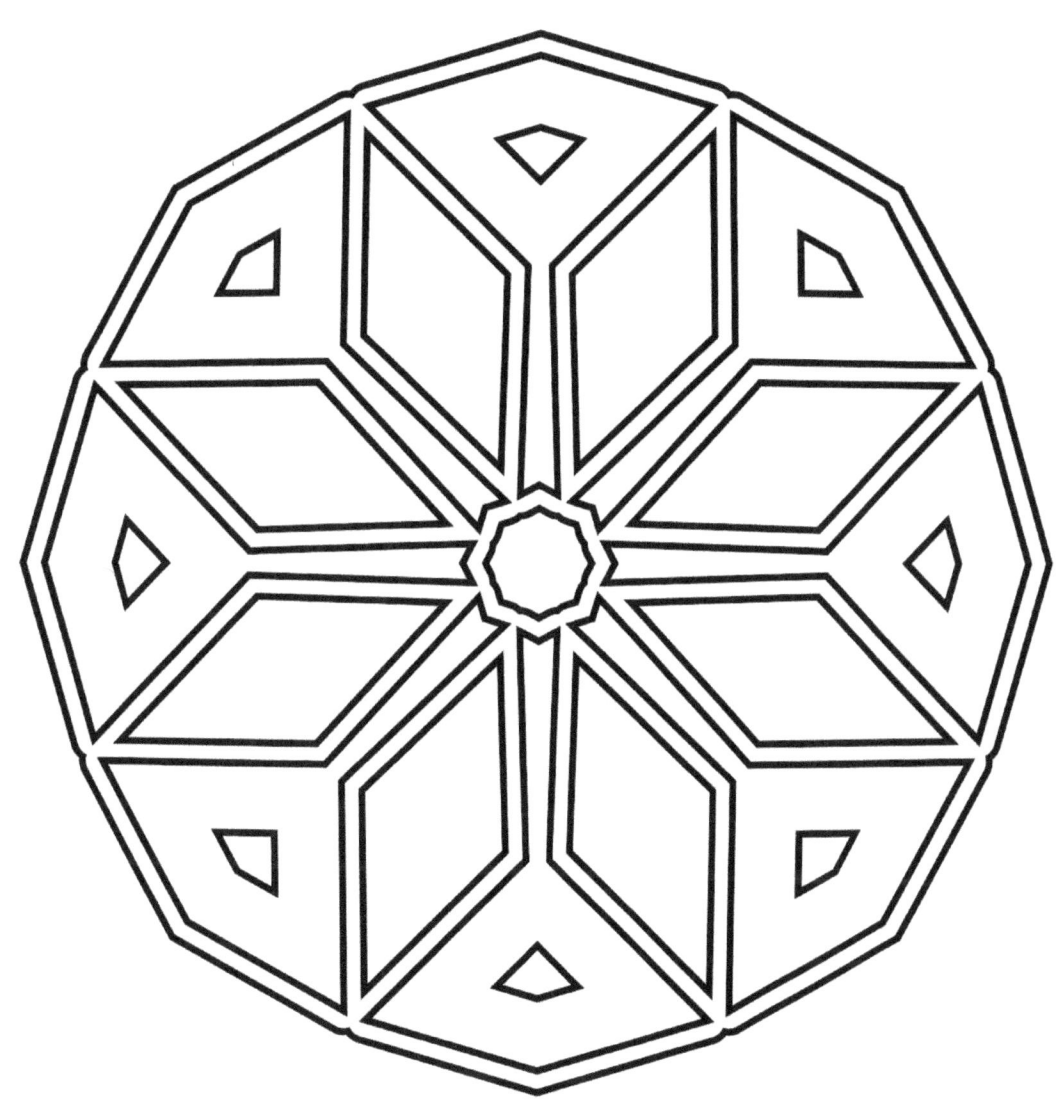

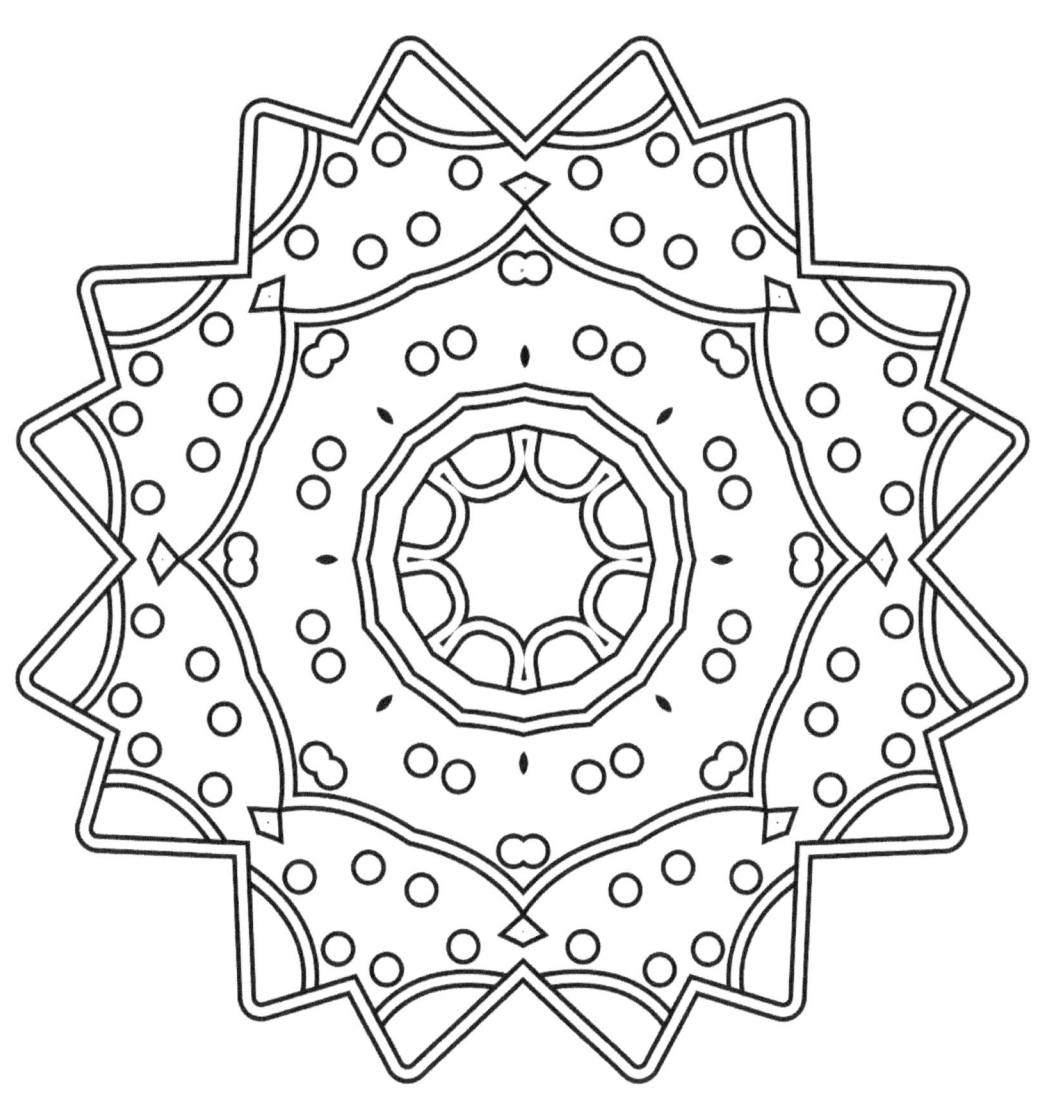

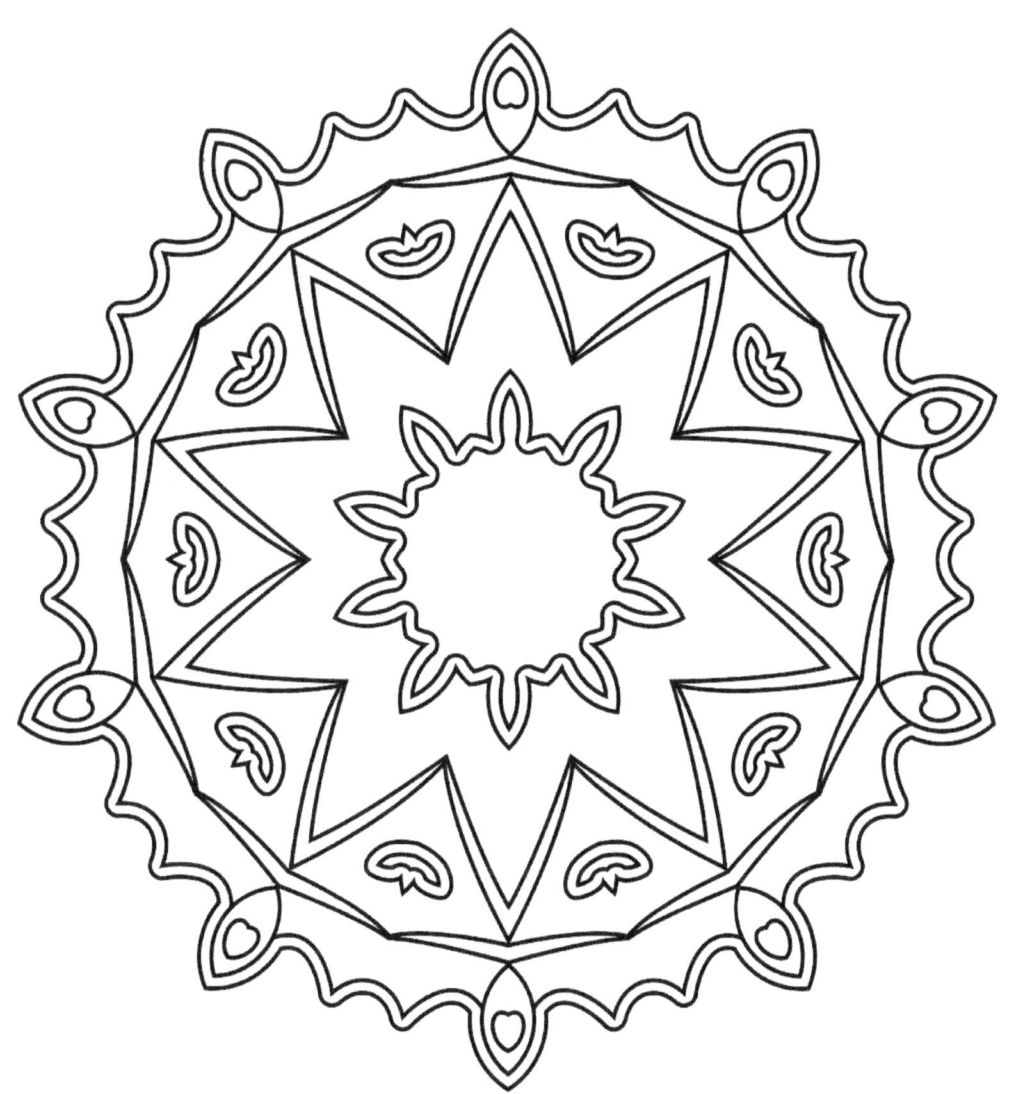

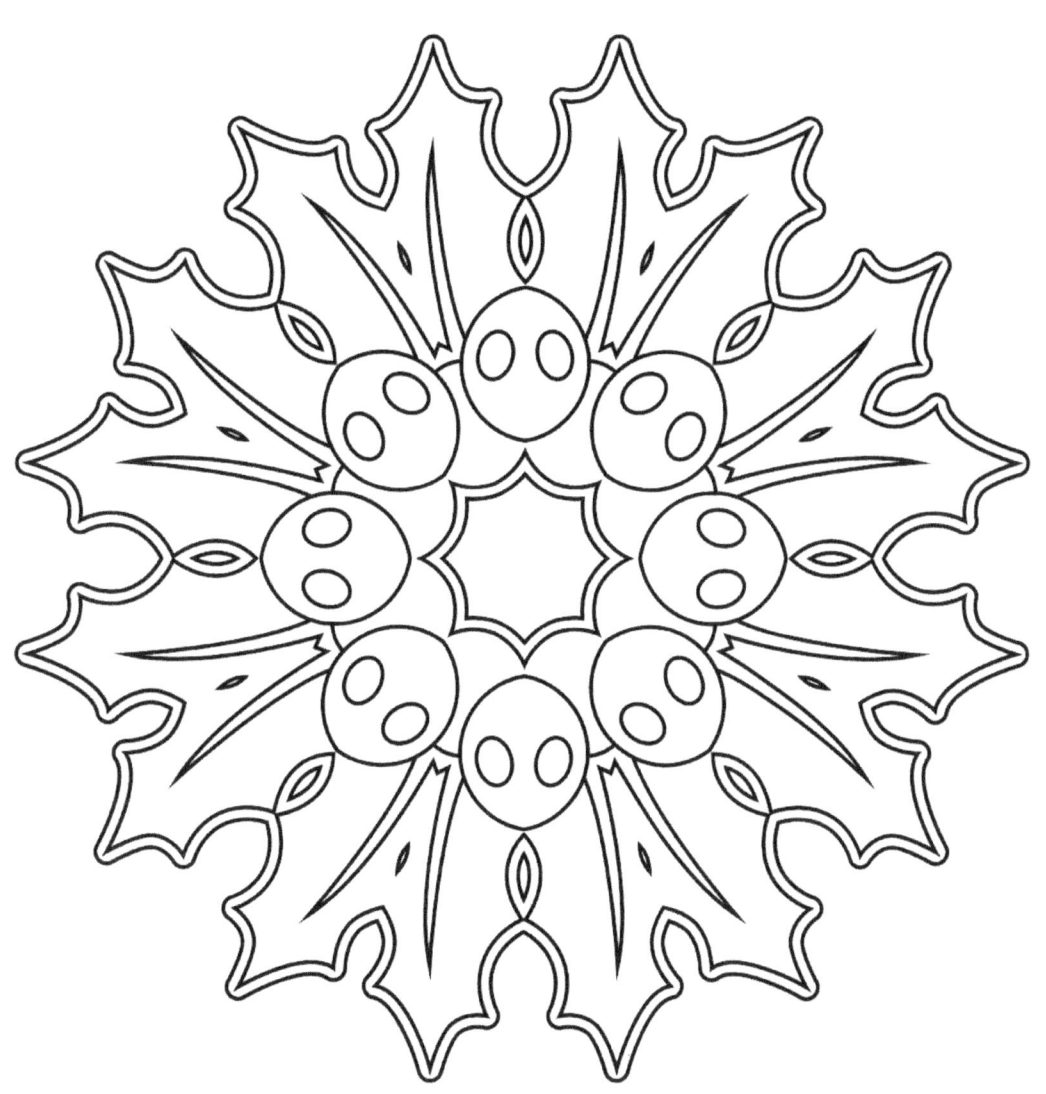

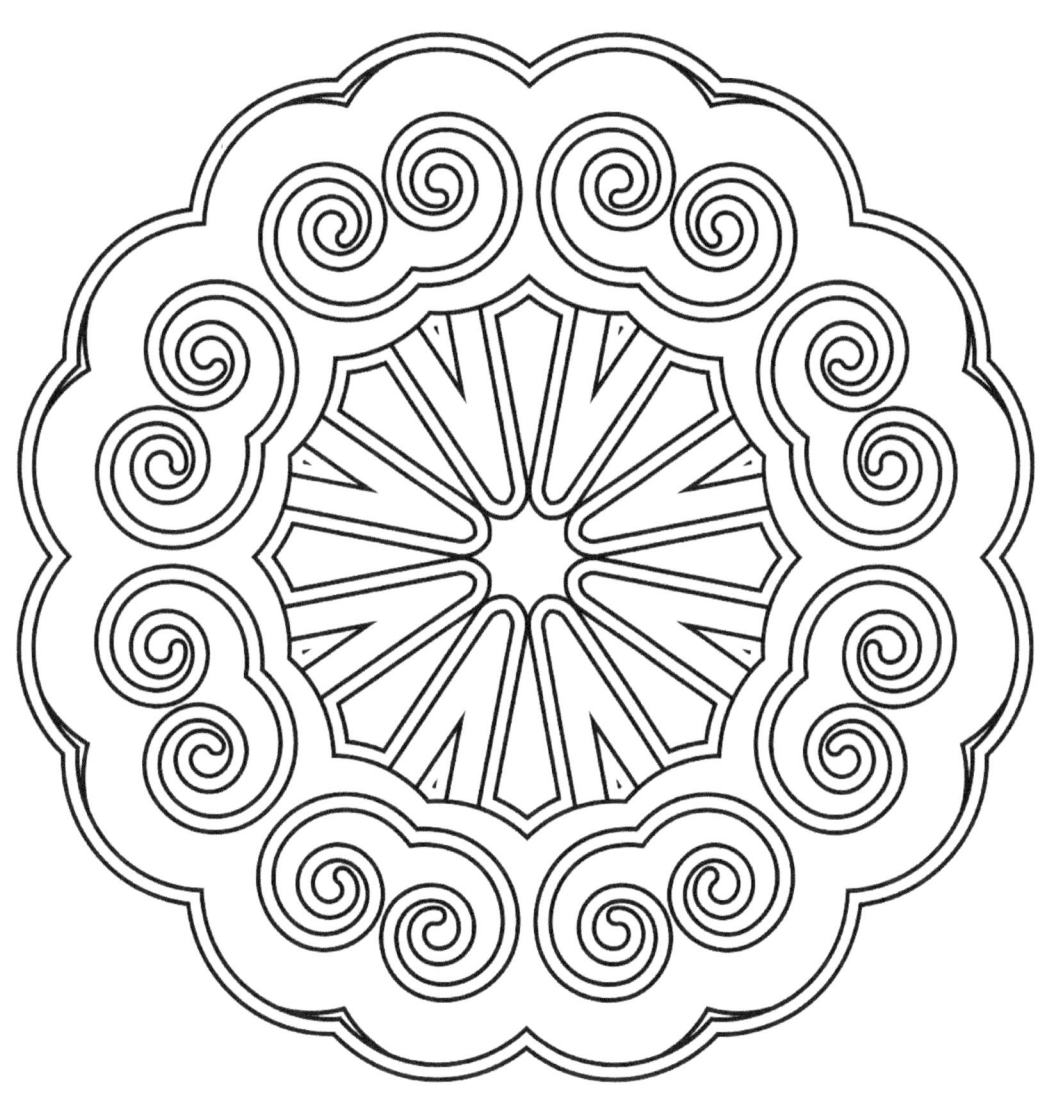

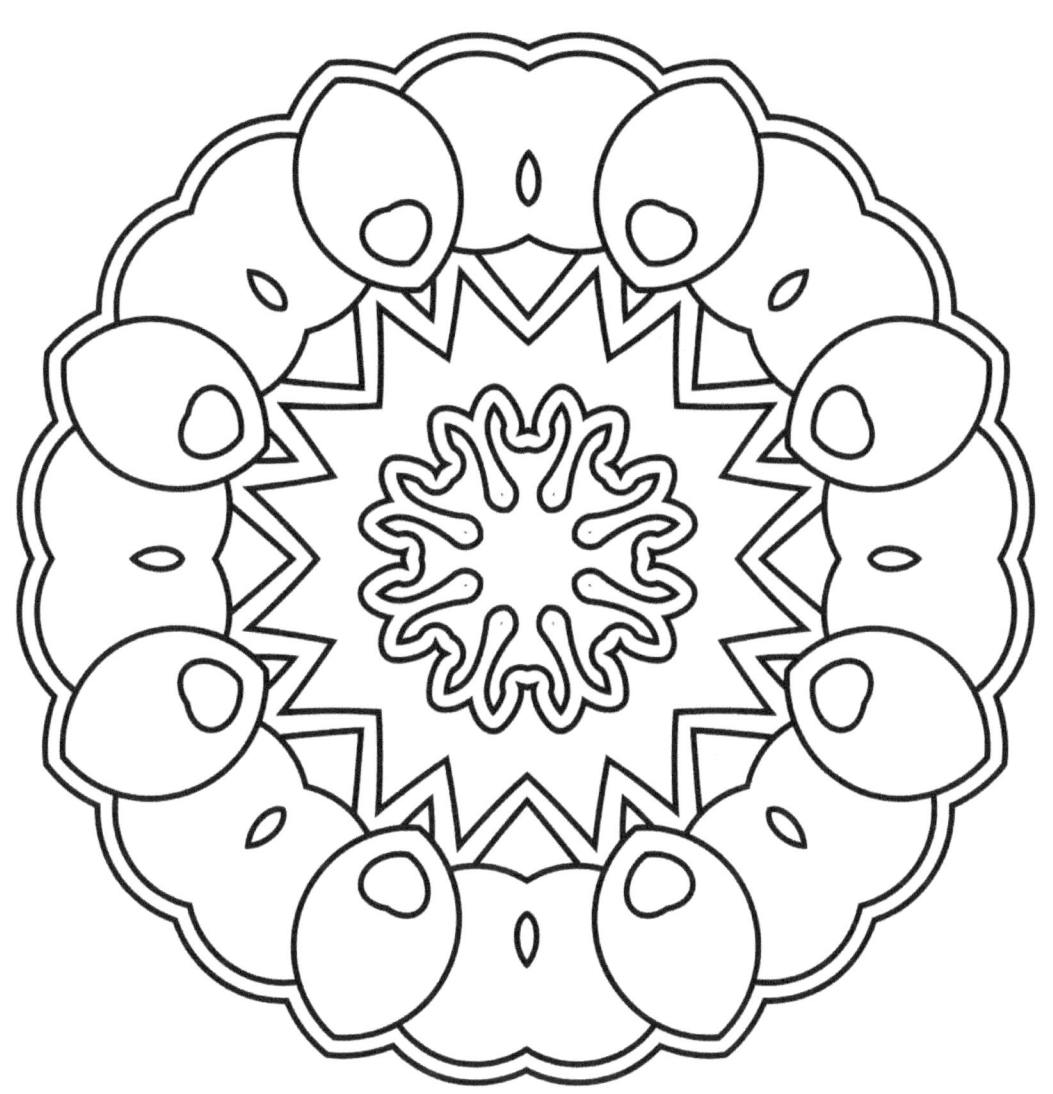

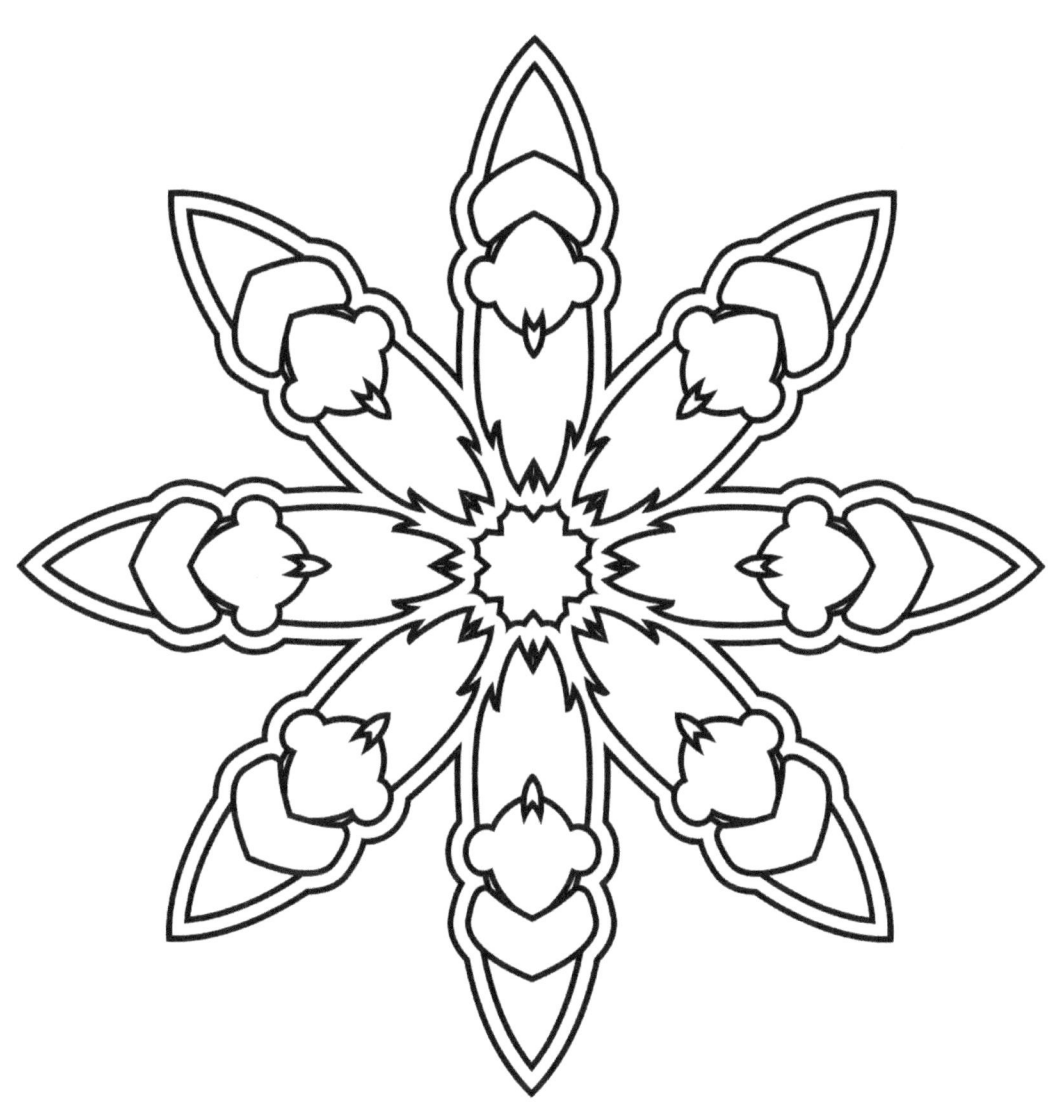

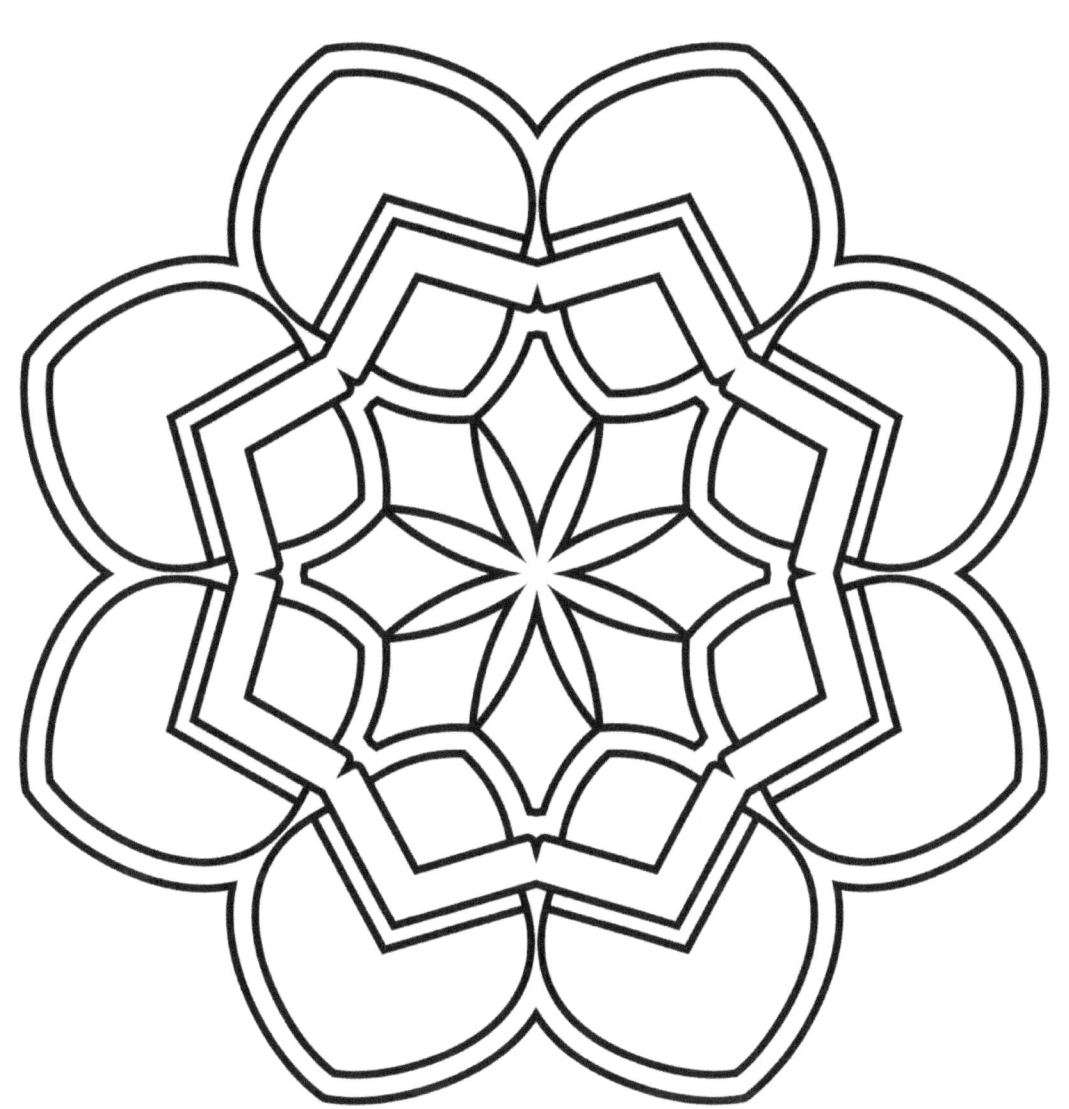

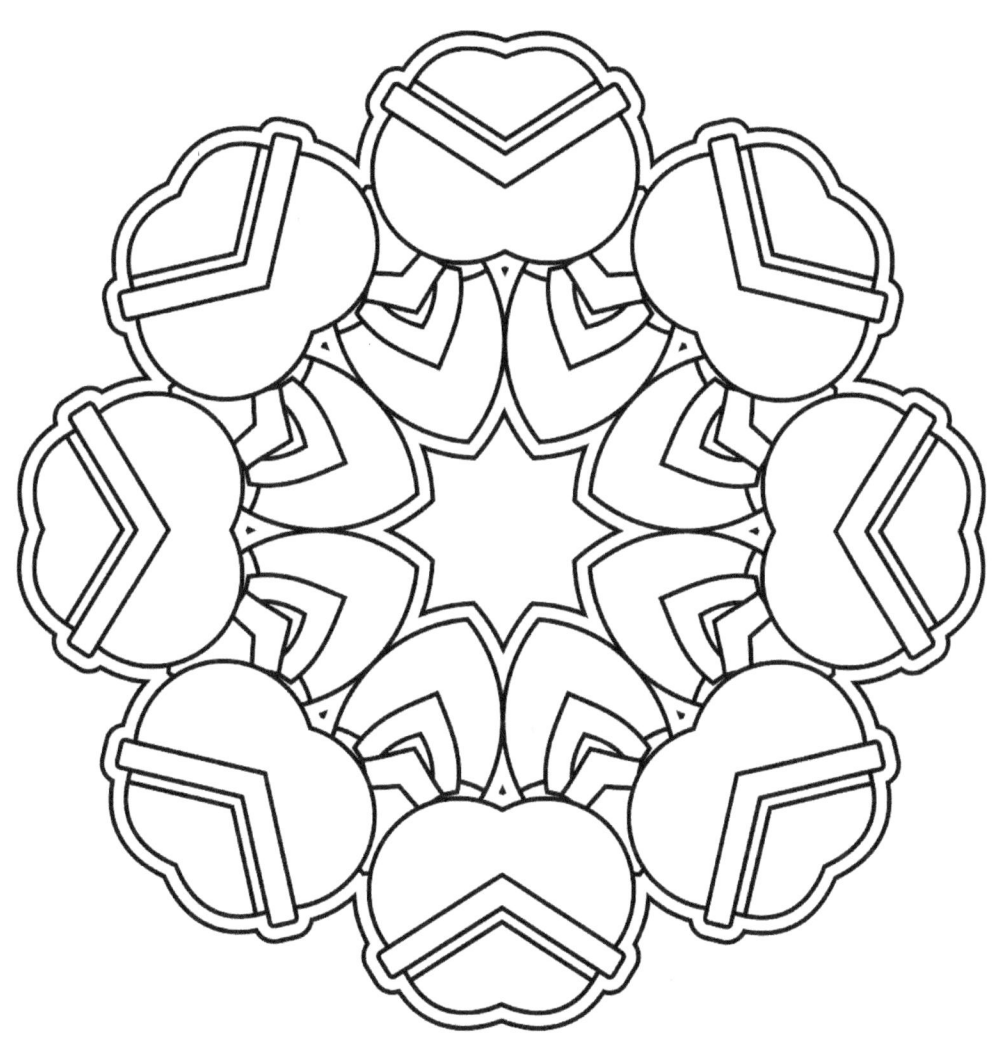

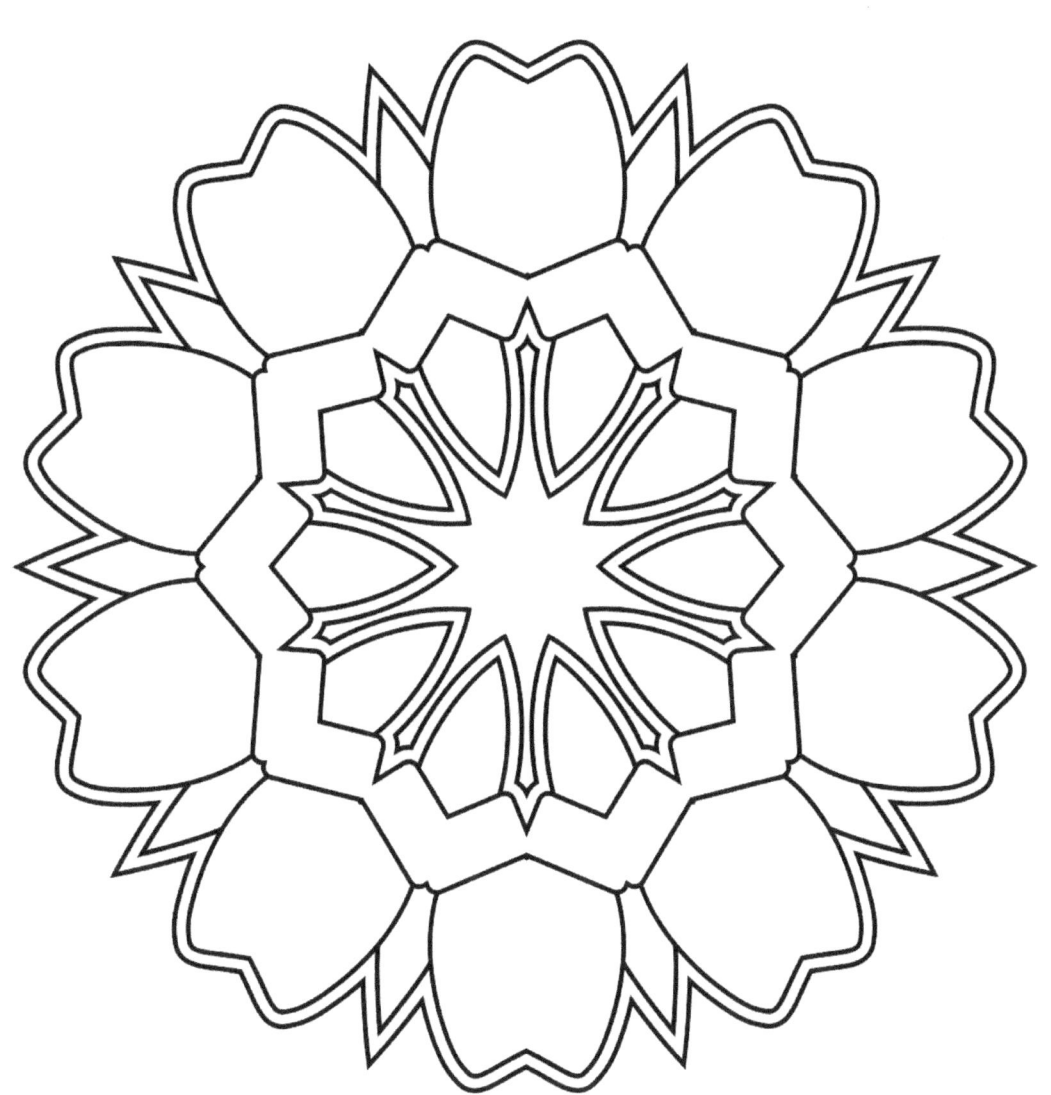

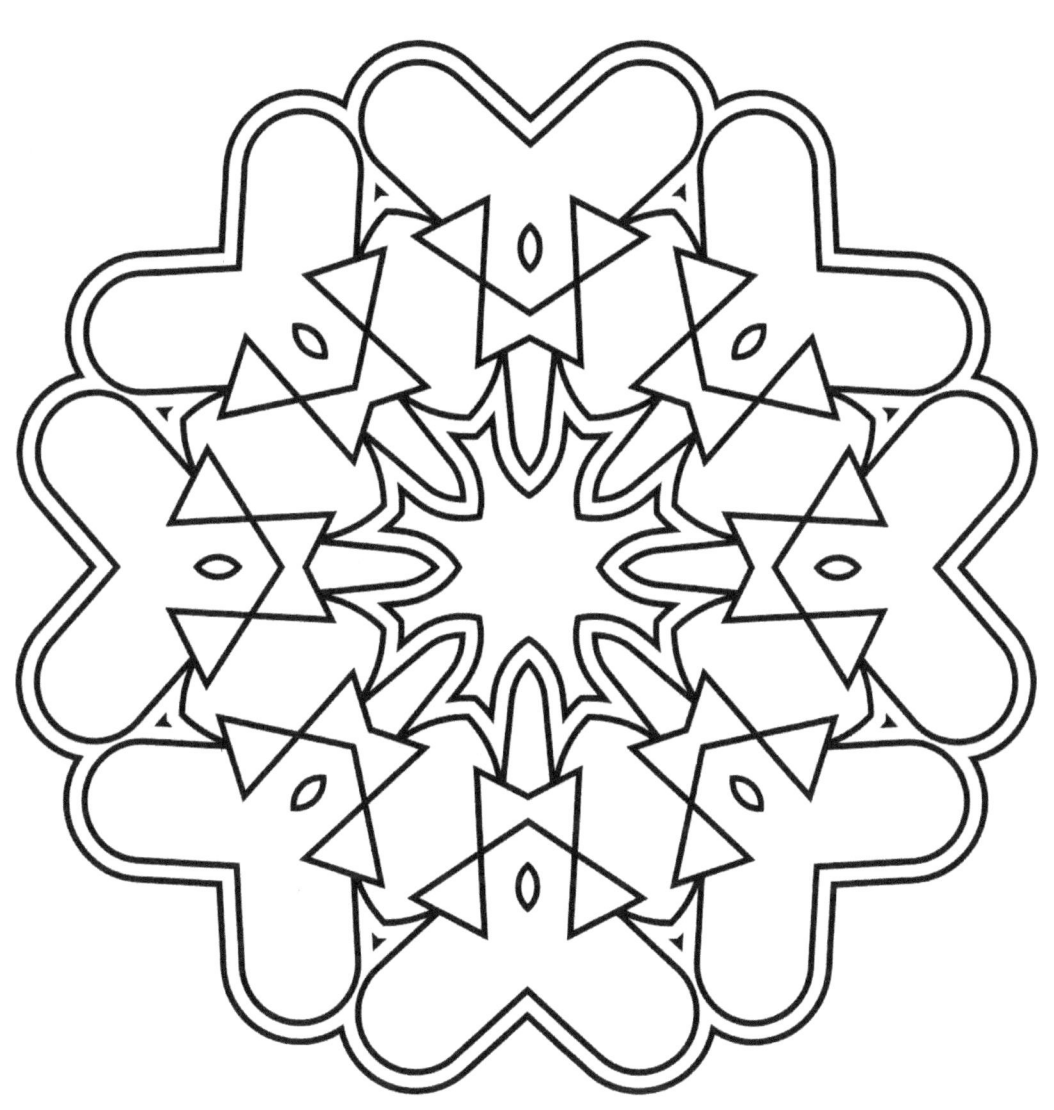

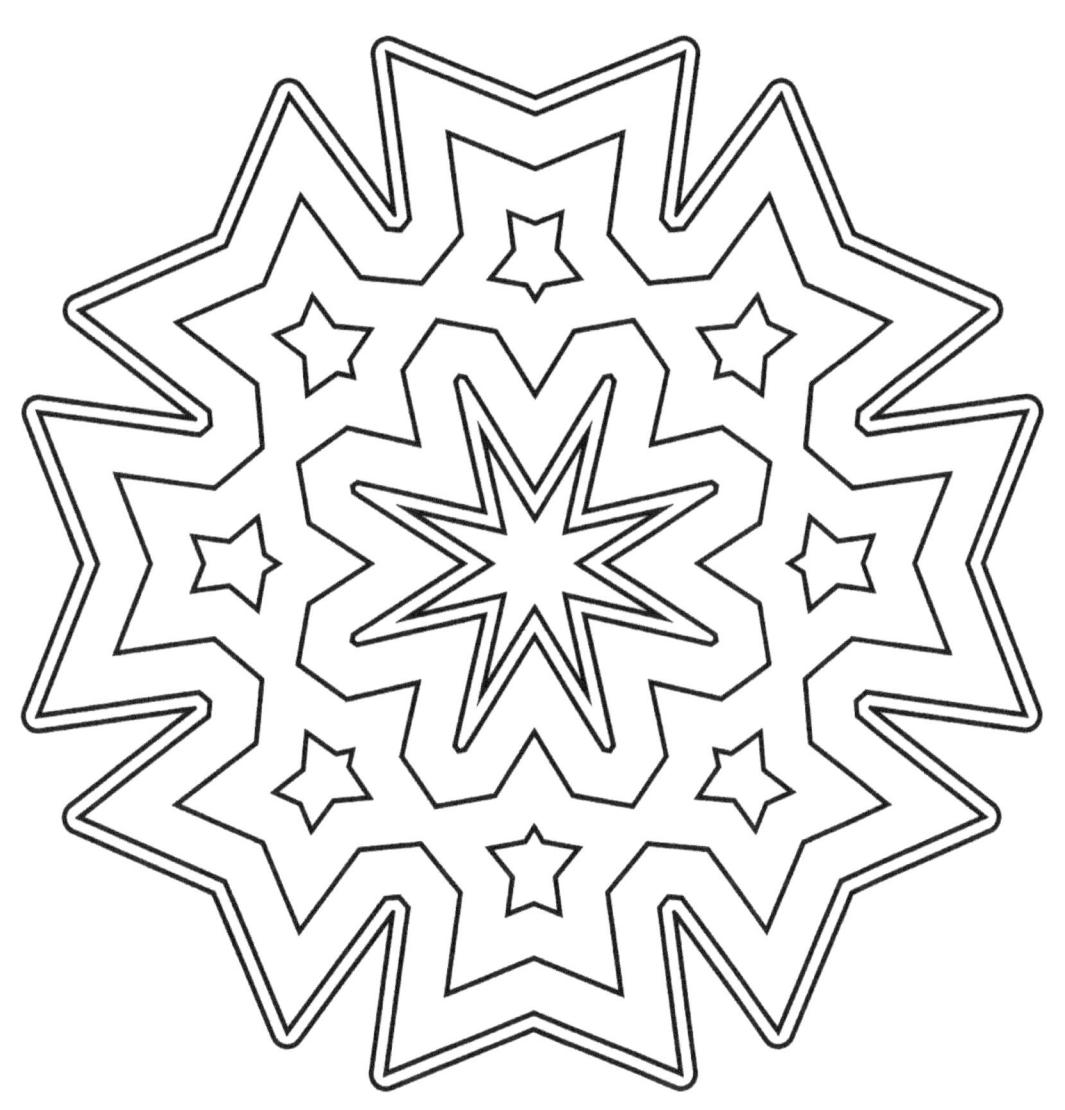

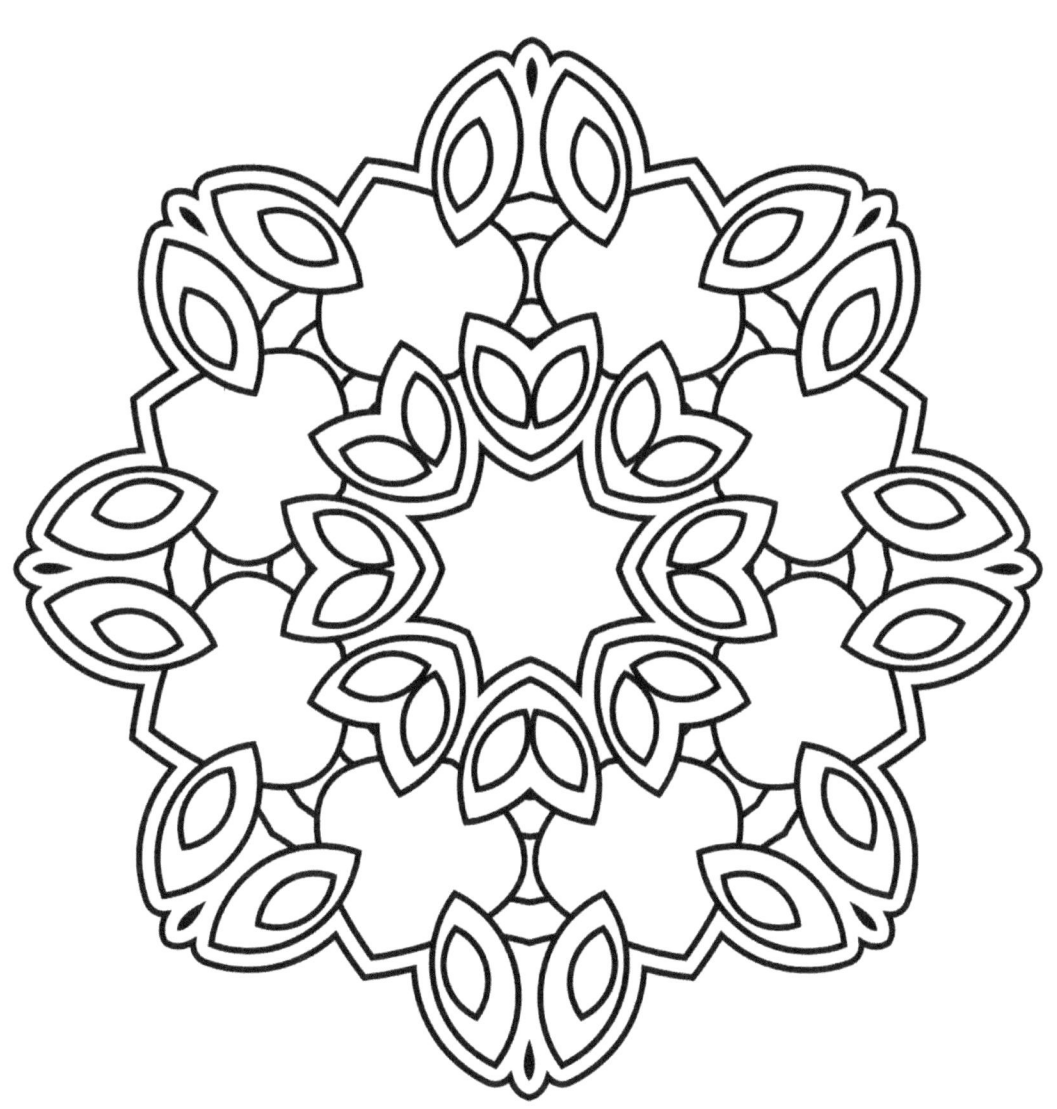

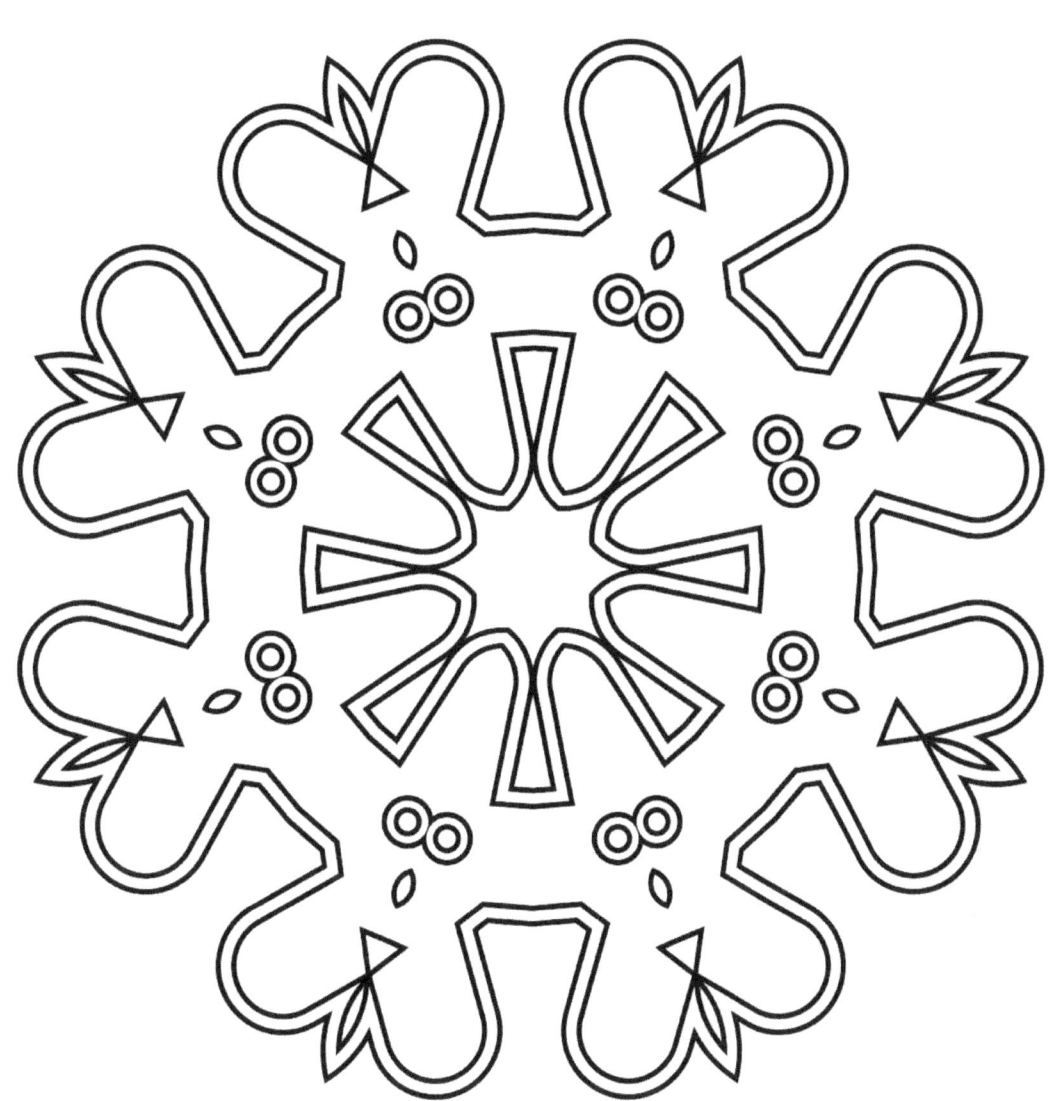

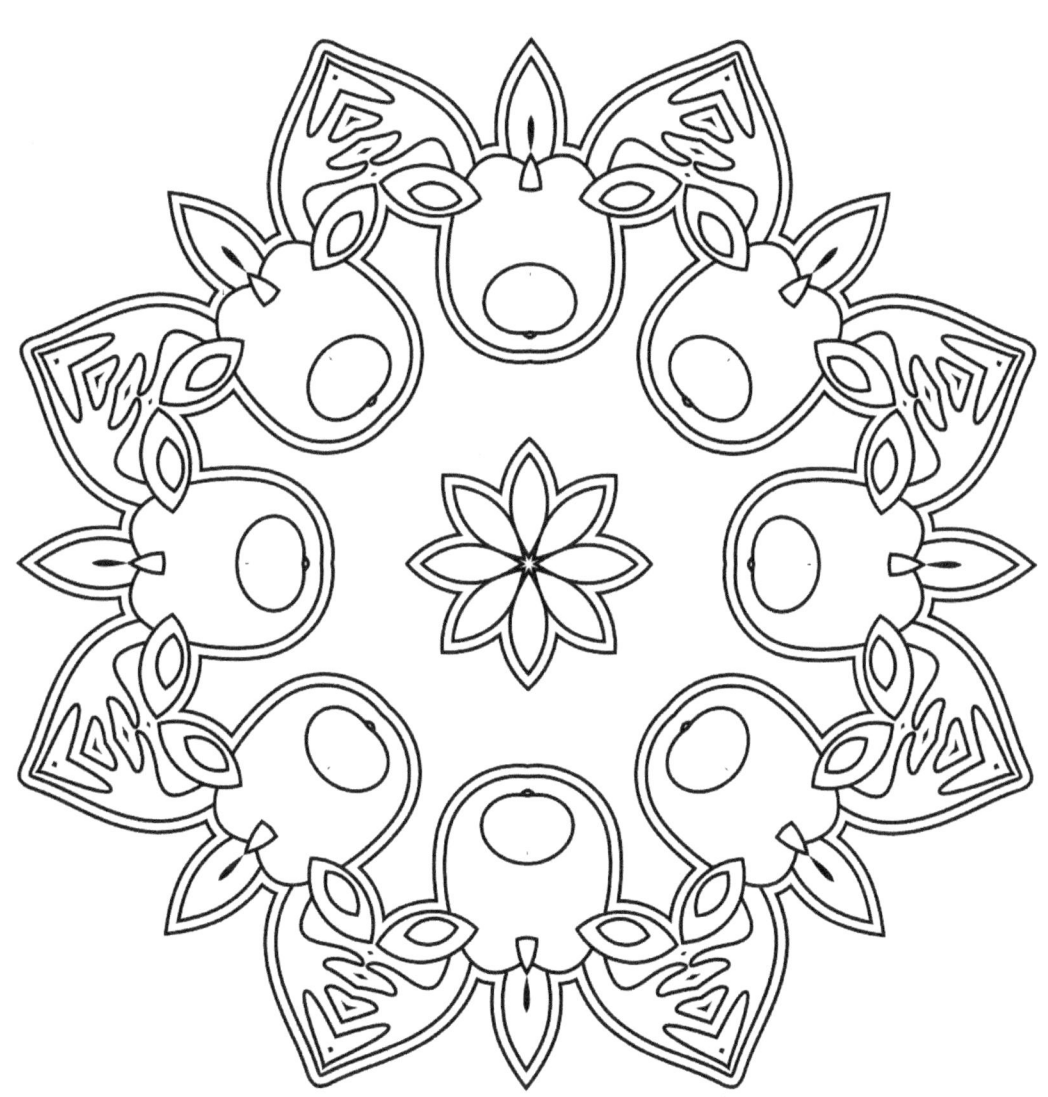

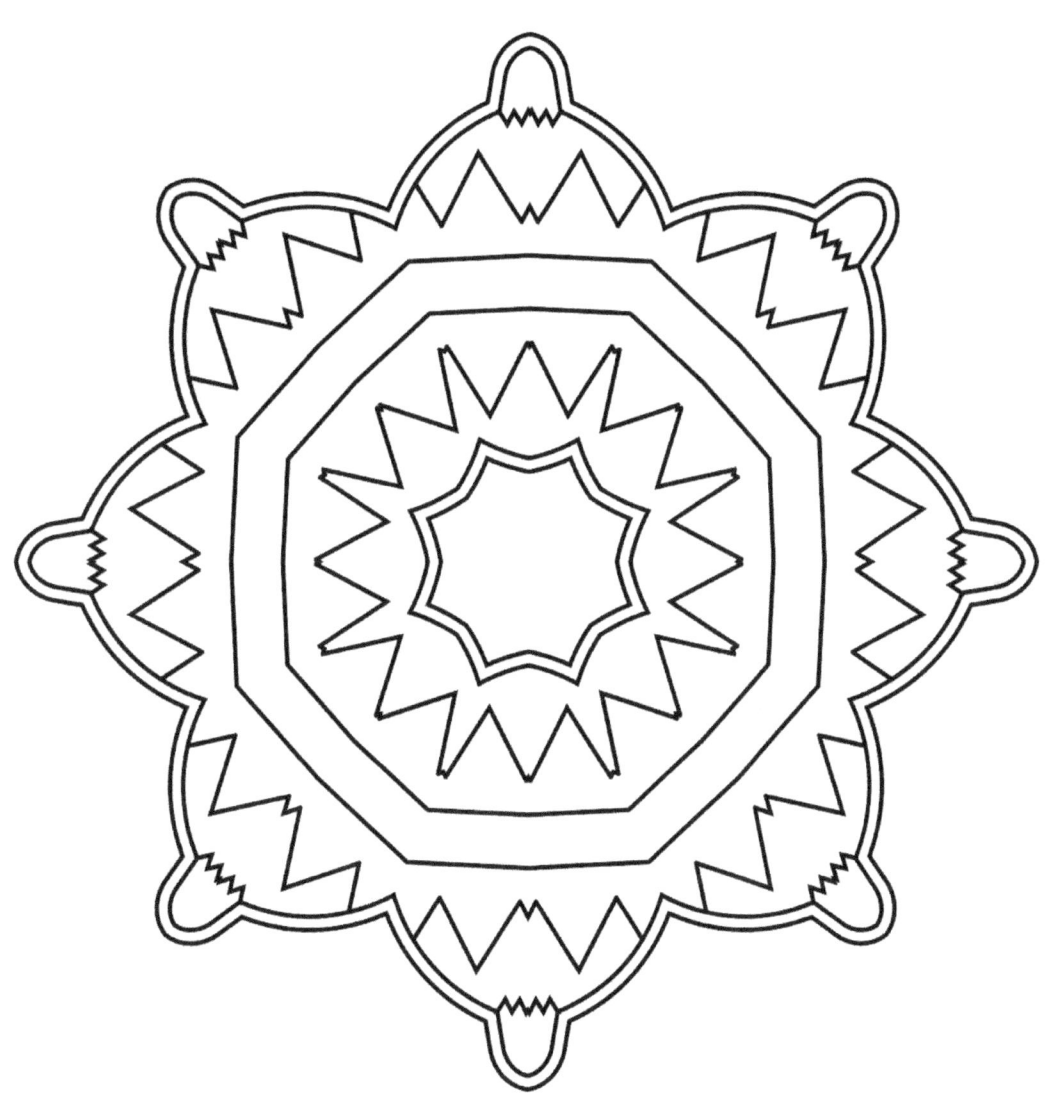

A Note About The Author

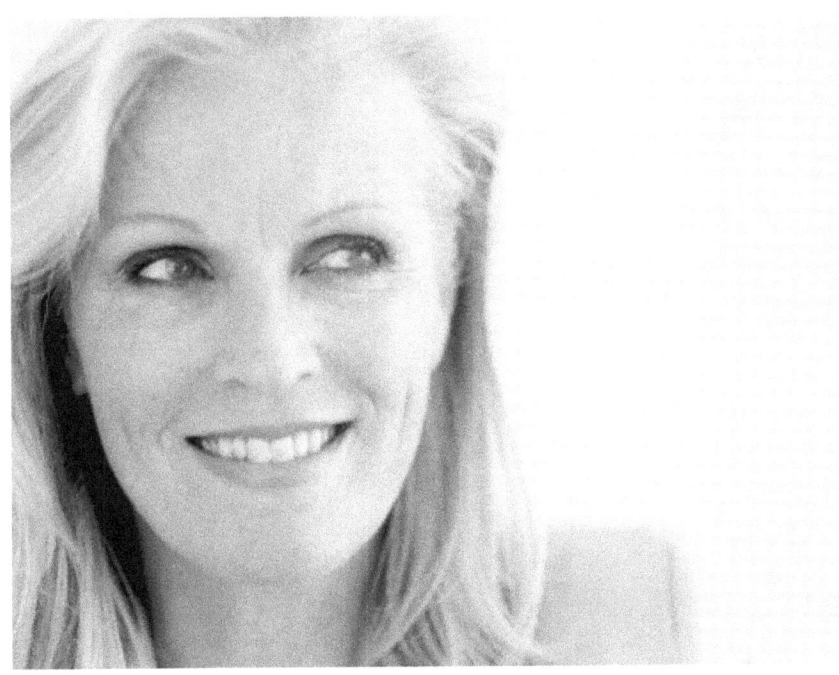

Belinda L. Frazier
Feel free to contact Belinda L. Frazier at belinda.coloring@gmail.com

Check out their Amazon profile here: http://www.amazon.com/-
/e/B01FSO94TA

www.ingramcontent.com/pod-product-compliance
Lightning Source LLC
Chambersburg PA
CBHW080635190526
45169CB00009B/3401